Tha

GW00771510

Through His Eyes

I hope you find love through these words. I hope
this book inspires you to love yourself because you
are special. You need to understand that.

May Allah guide you toward that which is best,
make your Dunya and your Deen easy for you.
Ameen.

If there is a word that you do not understand,
simply search the definition of the word on
Google.com.

e.g. "Define [word]"

fajrnoor.com.au

Through His Eyes

You look gorgeous today, especially
when you smile with those pearly whites,
even the angels start to blush at your beauty.

s.hukr

Through His Eyes

Honestly, you will just know.

You will be able to tell by his manners,
the way he looks at you. The way he talks
to you, pays attention to every single
word you say.

It will be in the way you make him smile.
In his laughter, his attention to every detail.

The atmosphere when he is around you.
A man who makes you a better woman,
a better sister, a better daughter and the
best future spouse.

. . .

Through His Eyes

You will realise he is right for you
when he makes you stronger emotionally,
physically and spiritually. He will empower
you; he will bring you closer to Jannah.

He will complete the half you are missing.
Be your teacher, your best friend, your
soulmate, your lover.

You will begin to realise that he will learn
to love you, just so you love yourself. You
will know he is right for you, the moment
he walks through those doors and your heart
finally finds peace in his presence.

s.hukr

Through His Eyes

You say you love deen
but run after Dunya.

You say you love to pray
but miss your Salah.

You say you love Allah
but spend time with Shaytan.

That's why I'm scared
when you say you love me.

s.hukr

Through His Eyes

Pulling a Muslim wife is so easy,
just wear a white thobe or a black kurta.

Speak with kindness. Display your values
through your character and conversation.

And make sure to leave her an honest yet
unique compliment that she won't ever forget.

If you can't do that naturally, then you need
to work on your relationship with Allah first.

s.hukr

Through His Eyes

Pulling a Muslim husband is so easy,
just become the most attractive woman
you can be.

A woman whose beauty isn't physical
appearance but beauty that softens every
man's heart who hears about you.

When you do meet a man who you find
comfort in, make sure his Deen and Character
meet the standards of Islam.

After you do your due diligence, you need to
drop him a hint of your interest in him.

Usually having a simple conversation
about marriage does the trick.

s.hukr

Through His Eyes

I would give you my heart, but you
already took it. Now give it back or
become my paradise.

s.hukr

Through His Eyes

If they asked me to describe
your beauty I'd say God has
poured moonlight into your soul.

s.hukr

Through His Eyes

You are the sea and I am the sky.

Nobody is in between, so when
would you like to meet?

s.hukr

Through His Eyes

You are mine and I am yours.
Now let me swim in your pretty
brown eyes and you can swim in
the valley of love hidden inside
my heart.

s.hukr

Through His Eyes

I loved her. Not simply but certainly.
and clearly, specifically; I loved her.
She was kind but warm. Her heart
was coloured by red roses.

She was everything a man would
desire and more.

A boy will not understand her value,
only a king would understand that
she is priceless gem from the heavens.

s.hukr

Through His Eyes

Hold my hand and
let's run to Paradise.

s.hukr

Through His Eyes

You are sweeter than honey,
more fragrant than musk.
You are the joy of my life and
I can't imagine life without you.

You are the smile of paradise,
your eyes are an ocean of beauty
and your heart is a valley of love.
I will cherish you forever.

You are my queen, the love of my life,
the mother of my children.
You are mine forever.

s.hukr

Through His Eyes

I DM'ed this Muslim girl and
called her sister. She got upset
and said I'm not your sister.

I said, if you don't want to be
my sister, I'll call you auntie
instead.

s.hukr

Through His Eyes

Your warmth and kindness is
more beautiful than you know.

It's my favourite thing about you.

s.hukr

Through His Eyes

Marry a soul you plan
on taking to Jannah.

s.hukr

Through His Eyes

If you can't treat her like a queen,
how will she treat you like a king?

s.hukr

Through His Eyes

When you smile at me,
my heart starts to race
like wind near the sea.

s.hukr

Through His Eyes

You must learn to love Allah first
before you learn to love me.

s.hukr

Through His Eyes

Trust is two way street.

If you expect it,
you have to give it.

s.hukr

Through His Eyes

I am jealous of a man who
may see your eyes by chance
and fall in love with them.

You are mine, only I can swim
in your eyes and choose to drown.

s.hukr

Through His Eyes

What is yours will always find
you but remember...

Destiny loves endeavour.

s.hukr

Through His Eyes

When you live for your soul
and not for seeking validation,
you become the vibe others are
searching for.

s.hukr

Through His Eyes

Did anyone tell you?

That if stealing wasn't haram,
I'd steal your heart and take
you to Jannah.

s.hukr

Through His Eyes

My heart is missing you,
so I mention your name in
my Duas in the hope that God
may unite us again.

s.hukr

Through His Eyes

The women in Jannah are jealous
of your beauty and it's about time
you accept the reality that Allah
doesn't make mistakes, he made
you the epitome of beauty.

s.hukr

Through His Eyes

A lot of problems can be solved just by
removing some food, some people, and
some habits from your life.

s.hukr

Through His Eyes

You know she has weak Eman
when she doesn't believe in Polygyny.

s.hukr

Through His Eyes

I don't want another pretty face to look at.

I don't want a marriage that becomes
another test for me.

I want a queen like my mother.
I want someone by my side,
whom I trust with my whole heart.

Someone who is the source of
blessings for me. She completes
me and I complete her, in Dunya
and in Deen.

I wanna marry someone who
I call my Slice of Paradise.

s.hukr

Through His Eyes

Her: "Why can't I see you?"

Him: "If you saw me, you wouldn't
stop daydreaming about me."

s.hukr

Through His Eyes

Her: "What are you looking at?"

Him: "Those pretty brown eyes that
I'll never get bored of."

s.hukr

Through His Eyes

I might have hoors in Jannah,
but you will forever remain the
Queen of my heart.

My love for you will make the
women in Jannah jealous.

s.hukr

Through His Eyes

I told you.

You look better with hijab.
Modesty is attractive to good men.

Your beauty is mine and
only I can fall in love with
you, over and over again.

s.hukr

Through His Eyes

Just like diamonds that are hidden beneath
layers of rock and dirt. It is the same with
righteous souls like you, that are hidden away
from everyone.

s.hukr

Through His Eyes

If I wanted to, I could make
your heart melt with soft kind
words that would bring a smile
to your face and warmth to your heart.

I have this gift with words and confidence that
doesn't stop me from doing as I please,
but I must put God first.

s.hukr

Through His Eyes

Men love differently.

We do not have to open up our hearts
and constantly show you the love inside.

We do our job by treating you like a
Queen as per the instructions given
by Allah.

Emotions do not get in the way of your
safety. We trust you to keep our family
together. We show affection by holding
your hand and walking towards Jannah.

s.hukr

Through His Eyes

How do I tell the angels that I miss you?
So they may rush to you and whisper
my name in your heart while you
make Dua for me?

s.hukr

Through His Eyes

Filters and makeup make you look
picture perfect, but I wanna fall in
love with your imperfections.

s.hukr

Through His Eyes

My wife is probably out there praying
Fajr alone and thinking about staying
single for life.

Sorry boo, Allah made us in pairs.

s.hukr

Through His Eyes

Men admire me and Women
want to be with me said
every great man.

But every great man admires the Prophet's
life and desire an eternity of happiness.

s.hukr

Through His Eyes

Don't you dare think about
cosmetic surgery. You don't
understand how beautiful you
are to me.

Don't you dare change the creation
of Allah, He has cursed those people.
You are a Queen. Period.

Do not argue with me.

s.hukr

Through His Eyes

I don't want to see a picture of you,
show me your heart, show me your soul.

Let me recognise my soulmate.
It ain't about the looks,
it's about the vibes.

s.hukr

Through His Eyes

Some people have reserved their
place in my heart long before I ever
meet them.

My heart knows what my
mind cannot explain.

s.hukr

Through His Eyes

You could be the most beautiful woman
in town but if you don't have Haya,
I won't find you attractive.
Capisce.

s.hukr

Through His Eyes

To my sisters that want to get married:

Never marry a man
who lies so easily.

Never marry a man
who does 50/50.

Never marry a man who
cannot control his anger.

Never marry a man who
neglects salah and knowledge
of the Quran and Sunnah.

Never marry a man until
you have discussed money.

Never marry a man until a
trusted man (brother / father)
deems him worthy of you.

Never marry a man who has
no haya in his eyes.

s.hukr

Through His Eyes

You can be a good girl with
a kind heart and still say "No".

As long as you are not opposing
the teachings of Islam.

s.hukr

Through His Eyes

It's not:
"What's your number?"

Its:
"How are you?"
"Are you okay?"
"I care about you."
"Tell me about your day."

s.hukr

Through His Eyes

I pray God grants me your soul
in this world but if not in this world
then forever in Jannah.

s.hukr

Through His Eyes

After our nikah, Imma cry
and thank Allah because you
are God's greatest gift to me.

I will treasure you forever.

s.hukr

Through His Eyes

Imagine being loved the way you love.

Now look at the first word.

s.hukr

Through His Eyes

She entered his heart and drowned
in a valley overflowing with love.

He saw the smile glowing on her face
and fell in love again.

s.hukr

Through His Eyes

If you are a good man don't talk
to women without merit, stay far away.

They will fall in love with you unintentionally.

s.hukr

Through His Eyes

Islam doesn't forbid a girl
from leaving the house.

It just requires her to be
accompanied by a bodyguard (mahram)
because that's how precious she is.

s.hukr

Through His Eyes

Pure love is when you love Allah
first and foremost and through that
love every person around you benefits.
They become closer to Allah because of you.

How can you not taste the sweetness
of love when you do things for
nobody but Allah?

s.hukr

Through His Eyes

I admire men who seem like their
only personality trait is loving their wife.

But I admire more the mothers who
raise kings. Without them this world
would be in chaos.

s.hukr

Women love differently.

I've come to the conclusion
that the reason males never
pick up on a woman's interest
is because they never do
things explicitly.

s.hukr

Through His Eyes

If you love that which Allah loves,
than how will Allah not grant you
that which you love?

s.hukr

Through His Eyes

Patiently waiting,
you are a drop in the ocean,
my love will devour you.

s.hukr

Through His Eyes

A pious woman helps bring
up a pious ummah and a
cursed woman will bring
up an unfortunate generation.

This is how important women
are in this world.

s.hukr

He Exists.
He doesn't drink.
He doesn't smoke shisha.
He doesn't dm random girls.
He doesn't play with someone's
feelings in the name of love.
He respects women.
Yes, He exists.

"Good women are for Good Men and
Good men are for Good women."

s.hukr

Through His Eyes

It is foolish to dream and hope for a perfect spouse who meets your every dot point. When you, yourself are a work in progress.

Do not hold other people to high level of morality and achievement when you, yourself are a complete waste of time.

s.hukr

Through His Eyes

In her smile,
I saw a glimpse of Paradise.
Seven billion smiles and
yours is my favourite.

When I want to smile,
I know exactly what to do,
I close my eyes and I think of you.

s.hukr

Through His Eyes

Don't wait for someone
to bring you flowers.

Plant your own garden and
decorate your own soul.

Someone will notice and
start helping you.

s.hukr

Through His Eyes

Some people win your heart
without even saying a word.
It was written.

s.hukr

Through His Eyes

You think that by wearing the Hijab
you become less attractive.

Tell me. How many poems do I need to
write to tell you that your Hijab makes you
more attractive in the eyes of God?

s.hukr

Through His Eyes

If her dad can't control what she wears,
what makes you think she'll change for you.

Don't waste your time bro.

s.hukr

Through His Eyes

Just because I don't agree with you,
doesn't mean I dislike you.

s.hukr

Through His Eyes

I'm an old soul with a young heart,
a vintage mind and an elegant tongue.

s.hukr

Through His Eyes

You have to live with you
for the rest of your life,
so why aren't you in
love with yourself?

s.hukr

Through His Eyes

Be such a good soul that
people crave your **vibes**.

s.hukr

Through His Eyes

I am mesmerised by your big,
beautiful eyes that scream for attention.

It only takes a glance, and you start to blush
and I start to smile. My heart softens and
love for you increases, and now that I have
your attention, go read some Quran.

s.hukr

Through His Eyes

When I see your smile,
the heavens and the stars
cease to exist, for in my mind,
your beauty is what remains.

My words cannot describe your
imperfect imperfections, I hope the
eternal flame of love will.

s.hukr

Through His Eyes

The Quran melts my heart
and tears start to flow down again.

Unconditional beauty enveloped
by words that touch my very soul.

Reminder of the inevitable truth that
every soul will taste **death**.

s.hukr

Through His Eyes

A women's love is plentiful,
but a man's love has depth.

Her love is wide like the ocean.
His love is deep like the ocean.

s.hukr

Through His Eyes

I want to be your favourite place
to go when you've had a bad day
or a good day.

s.hukr

Through His Eyes

Don't be sad because sad spelled
backwards is das und das ist nicht gut.

s.hukr

Through His Eyes

I whispered in her ear "I Love You".

And she said, "Repeat it in my other ear so I regain my balance".

s.hukr

Through His Eyes

Honey stop looking at your phone
for compliments, look at me.

Your eyes are full of language, they
are a novel that I adore reading, so
let me read them to you.

s.hukr

Through His Eyes

Three things of this world are very beloved to me: Peace, women and wisdom.

s.hukr

Through His Eyes

It's easy to love perfection but
I want to fall in love with
your imperfections...

s.hukr

Through His Eyes

You know I love you, that's why
I keep reminding you about **Salah**,
because I can't imagine Jannah
without you.

s.hukr

Through His Eyes

Islam gave women their rights
long before feminism did.

I am not a Feminist.
I am Muslim.

I follow the laws given
to us by God, not by men
or women of this world.

s.hukr

Through His Eyes

I await the day when your
smile brings me joy, your eyes
bring me ease and your beauty
melts my heart.

s.hukr

Through His Eyes

A woman who knows not of her beauty
is more beautiful than the one who
knows how beautiful she is.

Think deeply about what I said.

s.hukr

Through His Eyes

If you are my wife, I'm going to push you
to become a better person. I'm going to
support you with money, education, your
future, and goals.

I'm not going to put your success on pause
or distract you. My goal is to elevate your
mind, prosper with you.

After all you are my Wife and I want
you with me in Dunya and in Jannah.
Inshallah.

s.hukr

Through His Eyes

Her mindset will raise your children,
not her hijab or good looks.

So choose **wisely**.

s.hukr

Through His Eyes

Next time you feel ugly, remind yourself
that Allah took four oaths in the Quran
before stating He created you in the
best and most perfect form.

Your lord declared you the **epitome of
beauty**. How dare anyone make you think
otherwise.

s.hukr

Through His Eyes

If height mattered than the giraffe
would be the king of the jungle.

My king, make her laugh until
she forgets how short you are.

s.hukr

Through His Eyes

Marriage is like a business contract.
It is an exchange of benefits for both sides.

However, if you break the terms and
conditions that are written by Allah.
Then that marriage will become a test for you.

Every business goes up and down but not
every business goes through bankruptcy and
lawsuits.

s.hukr

Through His Eyes

If you want a marriage full of blessings,
invite a few, keep it small private
and avoid music.

Keep it to the sunnah.

Give charity if Allah has
blessed you with wealth.

s.hukr

Through His Eyes

You can be the immodest girl,
who guys look at and want more.

But never be the type of woman who
mistakes the hunger in a boy's eyes
for the passion in a mans.

s.hukr

Through His Eyes

Her eyes are a valley of mystery,
waiting to be read like a book.

s.hukr

Through His Eyes

Modesty is an element of a True woman.
She makes it known that she is not
eye candy for strangers.

That her value is more than what
appears in front of the eyes. She is
not afraid of anyone except Allah.
She is admired for her devotion.

s.hukr

Through His Eyes

I ask Allah for you twice.

Once in this Dunya and
forever in Jannah.

s.hukr

Through His Eyes

I love looking into your pretty eyes,
I adore them, they never age because
they are the windows to your soul.
What a beautiful soul you have.

You awaken the strength inside of me to
keep going. This world is meaningless
without your existence. You are the
definition of love that never ends.

My heart might be a valley of love
but it's your eyes that are an ocean of
perpetuating beauty.

s.hukr

Through His Eyes

If I was not commanded to
lower my gaze, I would have
fallen in love just by staring
at you.

I lower my gaze not because
you aren't beautiful but because
I fear Allah.

s.hukr

Through His Eyes

I am nothing but a sinner,
if you knew my list of sins,
you would never befriend me…

but if you saw my list of deeds
you would fall in love and forget
about my sins.

s.hukr

Through His Eyes

When you start your day with Fajr,
your face starts to glow with Noor.

You don't need makeup, you just need
a splash of Noor every morning.

s.hukr

Through His Eyes

When you live for your soul and
not for seeking validation, you
become the vibe others are
searching for.

s.hukr

Through His Eyes

Love yourself enough to set
boundaries. To know that your
time and energy are precious.

But never let pride enter the heart.

s.hukr

Through His Eyes

Good men take care of their sisters,
being her best friend, playing with her,
making her laugh, spending quality time
with her.

Being there for her in good and bad times,
encouraging the Hijab, Salah, righteousness
and addressing her doubts and fears.

Being her bodyguard against the world,
because she is a princess.

s.hukr

Through His Eyes

Honestly when Allah wants two hearts to
meet, he will make both of them move.

s.hukr

Through His Eyes

Men are not wallets.
Women are not toys.

Why do you treat one
another like objects?

s.hukr

Through His Eyes

Honey…

You are beautiful.
You don't need filters or makeup.
Because your heart is good.

I know this because every time,
I look into your eyes, I drown
in an ocean of beauty.

s.hukr

Through His Eyes

Everyday my heart thinks of new ways
to make you closer to Allah, so He would
increase the love between us.

s.hukr

Through His Eyes

Don't tell women they are beautiful. They already get told that too many times and frankly they don't need to know that. Their value isn't tied to their beauty alone.

Instead tell them something unique, something from the depths of your heart. Something that doesn't make them forget who you are.

And always leave women with some gesture of kindness that may inspire a Dua from their heart. A woman's Dua is very valuable, don't ever forget that.

Your words should inspire them to make Dua for you and through that you will receive Barakat in your life.

s.hukr

Through His Eyes

My eyes are blind to everyone else but you,
even though I have never seen you.

My heart is always in search for you, even
though, I am not worthy of you,
but ever am I grateful.

s.hukr

Through His Eyes

Mountains can collapse,
the sky may fall but the
beauty you have only
increases when I'm
with you.

s.hukr

Through His Eyes

We could be married for 10 years
but if she came back into my life,
I would marry her too.

s.hukr

Through His Eyes

If you forget your salah, then
I don't like you.

Lovers don't forget, we always
remember the beloved.

s.hukr

Through His Eyes

A diamond ring doesn't make a queen.
She is the gem.

Money doesn't make a king,
It is his character.

s.hukr

Through His Eyes

I will have patience with you,
but modesty is necessary.

I won't let the devil get to you.
You deserve Paradise. You must
accept the Hijab sincerely.

Hijab is not a choice,
it is not a journey,
it simply compulsory.

Hijab is **Compulsory** for every
Muslim Woman who wants Jannah.

s.hukr

Through His Eyes

The abandoned city in my
heart is lit up with your kindness.

We men go through a lot, more than you can
imagine. O women don't forsake us kindness.

s.hukr

Through His Eyes

She asked me: "What is the difference
between me and the moon?"

So I replied: "The difference, my love, is that
when you smile, I forget about the moon."

s.hukr

Through His Eyes

Allah doesn't give us what we want
He gives us what we need...

So you have an eternity of what
you desire.

s.hukr

Through His Eyes

They asked:
"What makes people so inclined to you,
yani you're not handsome, you're not rich,
you're a simple man?"

Simple Man:
"If you are loved by God, how can you
not be loved by his people?"

s.hukr

Through His Eyes

They said:
Why are you crazy about her?
You haven't even met her!

I replied:
Who says that I have never met her? She has been
in my soul for centuries. 50,000 years before the
creation of the sea and the sky, Allah wrote her
name next to mine.

s.hukr

Through His Eyes

Life is short.
Text him first.

You literally have nothing to lose,
you either get a king or
he doesn't get a queen.

s.hukr

Through His Eyes

I pray you fall in love with someone
who never stops choosing you and
I hope you feel at home when you
look at Him.

s.hukr

Through His Eyes

I pray you enter Jannah because
It wouldn't be Jannah without you.

s.hukr

Through His Eyes

Don't ever steal a women's heart,
it was never made to be stolen,
rather, ignite it with undying
flames of love.

s.hukr

Through His Eyes

Be yourself, if you don't like yourself,
then improve and grow into a version
of yourself that you admire.

s.hukr

Through His Eyes

Let's meet for a cup of coffee
and dream of better days.

s.hukr

Through His Eyes

She was beautiful, but not like
those women in magazines.

She wasn't beautiful for something
as temporary as her looks.

She was beautiful for the way she
thought, her heart was pure,
there was Haya in her eyes.

She didn't need makeup; her face
was already glowing with Noor.

...

Through His Eyes

She was beautiful for the sparkle
in her eyes when she talked about
something she loved. She was a
blessing from Allah.

She was the reason why
the angels would surround us.

She is my Slice of Paradise.

s.hukr

Through His Eyes

Did anyone tell you?
That your Noor is so bright,
it hides your imperfections
with radiating beauty?

Well now you know why
I admire you so much.

s.hukr

Through His Eyes

Be the kind of soul that others
wish they could meet a thousand times.

s.hukr

Through His Eyes

You can have a wedding with a
handsome guy and a pretty girl,

but I much rather see a beautiful marriage
with a faithful man and a pious woman.

s.hukr

Through His Eyes

Men who marry for only beauty and
Women who marry for only money
are equally robbed in the end.

s.hukr

Through His Eyes

A man without a wife,
is still a boy and a woman
without a man is still a girl.

They have yet to taste sacrifice, love,
commitment, trust and bundles of joy.

s.hukr

Through His Eyes

My home will be a home with no loud anger,
no explosive rage, no slamming doors or
breaking glass, no name calling, shaming
or blackmail. My home will be gentle,
it will be warm.

It will keep my loved ones safe.
A place of peace, love, patience and Deen.

s.hukr

Through His Eyes

Be sweet even when others are sour,
you have no idea what they are going through.

s.hukr

Through His Eyes

Your children will follow
your example, not your advice.

s.hukr

Through His Eyes

How lucky are you to meet someone
who is loved by Allah?

What an honour to be in the vicinity of
someone whose heart doesn't forget the
remembrance of Allah?

Whoever is given divine gifts from Allah
must be someone worthy of Jannah.

O how I wish, we meet again and that you
never leave my life again.

s.hukr

Through His Eyes

Prayer is invisible so is love,
when they are both are absent from
our life, we are left to feel miserable.

s.hukr

Through His Eyes

If you disobey Allah for the sake
of someone you love.

Just remember, the one whom
you love, is in the control of the
one whom you disobey.

s.hukr

Through His Eyes

I hope you don't find what you're
looking for. Rather, I wish that
God guides you to whatever is
best for you.

We humans tend to desire things
that end up hurting us, but God
intends the absolute best for us.
So trust Him.

s.hukr

Through His Eyes

May Allah give your heart and mind
ease and put you to sleep such that
you wake up with Noor upon Noor
glowing from your face.

s.hukr

Through His Eyes

This body of mine is private property.
He has only meant it for my spouse to see.
So how can I just give any stranger it's
accessibility?

s.hukr

Through His Eyes

Your beauty cannot be measured
from how you appear. It is your heart
that I fell in love with.

Every time I see you, I am reminded
that Allah blessed me with a heart that's
close to Him.

There is light shining from your face that I
cannot describe. When I look at you, I feel
happiness, as if I am already in Paradise.

s.hukr

Through His Eyes

Mixing culture and religion is where
a lot of Muslims go wrong.

s.hukr

Through His Eyes

As men,
Allah made women beloved to us,
they may test our sabr, our manhood,
our loyalty, but we will still love them
because they are a part of us.

s.hukr

Through His Eyes

A pretty girl means nothing to me,
but a woman who inspires me to be
a better man, now that's what I call
wifey material.

s.hukr

Through His Eyes

Fill the void in your life with the love of Allah.
Don't claim love, if you disobey the beloved.

Lovers are obedient to those whom they love.

s.hukr

Through His Eyes

How is it?

That when I see you smile…

All my pain disappears, only love remains.

s.hukr

Through His Eyes

I have heard that she stays awake at night.
Tell her I don't sleep either.

I have heard that she cried silently.
Tell her that I don't laugh either.

I have heard that she remembers me.
Tell her that I didn't forget too.

I have heard that she claims to be loyal.
Tell her that I am also not unfaithful.

s.hukr

Through His Eyes

When you meet people assume the best in them, don't go looking for mistakes because you will find them.

Rather, look for potential because every soul has the potential for something great.

s.hukr

Through His Eyes

A wife of another nationality is like a translated poem. Learn to read the eyes and you'll understand her heart.

s.hukr

Through His Eyes

The most beautiful women that I have ever
met on the face of the earth, have always
been hidden behind a veil of light.

Consider yourself lucky
if you ever meet one.

s.hukr

Through His Eyes

I might be ugly.

But I'll make you feel butterflies
every morning, take you on adventures
every evening and you can keep the
keys to my heart for eternity.

s.hukr

Through His Eyes

All these girls want to get married but
keep waiting like lost sheep.

I thought Muslim women were Queens,
who weren't afraid to propose if they ever
found a king. I hope I'm not wrong.

s.hukr

Through His Eyes

People are so hard to please.
I gave up a long time ago.

s.hukr

Through His Eyes

Far beyond the chaos of Dunya, I'll
wait for you in this hidden valley I
call love. Hold my hand and let me
read your eyes. I want to melt your
heart and touch your soul.

s.hukr

Through His Eyes

Valentine's Day.

You show off your love
once a year, but love was
never assigned a day.

Why do I see Muslims
follow pagan traditions?

Follow the beauty of Islam.
Perfected fourteen hundren years ago.

s.hukr

Through His Eyes

It's so rare to find a Muslim family
that actually follows Islam, instead
of culture that contradicts Islam.

Now read that again.

s.hukr

Through His Eyes

You must repent as soon
as you sin for death does
not wait for your repentance.

We all sin but the best of
us are those that repent
sincerely.

s.hukr

Through His Eyes

As a woman, you are loyal to
your man as long as he is loyal to Allah.

As long as your man is not opposing Islam,
you must stay by his side even if he may seem
wrong and foolish. He will learn and grow
with time.

You job is to support him in way he will
understand and not burden him.

s.hukr

Through His Eyes

Women love to talk but some
women need a mute button.

They speak with unnecessary emotions
that drive away your patience.

s.hukr

Through His Eyes

My future wife probably out there
struggling with hijab, boo I ain't
coming until you wear it.

I want a wifey with Haya.

s.hukr

Through His Eyes

She isn't looking for riches, beauty or poetry. She is looking to be understood, respected and loved.

Respect is how you attract her, understanding her will give her security and love will make her yours forever.

Why are guys so dumb and selfish?

s.hukr

Through His Eyes

And when a man talks from
his heart and his tongue doesn't lie,
he speaks poetry.

s.hukr

Through His Eyes

My old soul is tired.

Not from my age but
my time away from you.

I miss you deeply.

s.hukr

Through His Eyes

If I ever benefited you,
remember me in your Duas.

s.hukr

Through His Eyes

It would only take me a heartbeat
to capture your glowing smile, read
your pretty eyes, learn your beautiful
language and make you forever mine.

Because I come from a family who
is fluent in love.

s.hukr

Through His Eyes

My love, once I find you, I will treasure you like a gem from the heavens because you are God's greatest gift to me. I will give you half my heart and the other half is for Allah.

I will move mountains for you, bring you peace after every hardship and comfort you to the best of my ability but never let your ego interfere with God's plan.

s.hukr

Through His Eyes

A good man will not value your makeup, your fake lashes or nails. Some of which are clearly forbidden. He will not value your exterior beauty as much as he will value your Haya.

He will not value your ability to earn like he does. Rather he will value your ability to maintain and handle business inside the house.

He will value your Eman, your obedient nature and the way you push him to become a better man. He will value your ability to be a great wife and a great mother. That's valuable.

s.hukr

Through His Eyes

I've met plenty of men my age,
but most seem boring to me.
We all think relatively the same way.

However, for every hundred I meet,
I find a man amongst them whose
vibe I actually enjoy and admire.

s.hukr

Through His Eyes

My love for this world is as temporary
as this world is to me. But my love for
you is eternal, just as you are to me.

s.hukr

Through His Eyes

Idk why Muslims have such big luxurious
weddings. There is absolutely no Barakat, no
humbleness, no modesty, no sense of Sunnah.

They spend all this money and effort telling people
about their marriage that just began without any
guarantee that it will not end in a divorce. They
celebrate like the westerns and expect no
punishment from Allah. May Allah guide you
hypocrites.

I would rather invest in my marriage or go on a
honeymoon with my wife than have a luxurious
wedding with people who I barely know.

s.hukr

Through His Eyes

I went to the shore to forget about you, but
the wet sand was the colour of your hair, and
the sea was the colour of your eyes. The wind
carried your smell, and the sun was as bright as
your smile. There was nowhere I could go that
wouldn't remind me of you.

s.hukr

Through His Eyes

If I ever get married, Imma post pictures
of the sky and act like nothing happened.

During the night, I'll wakeup and thank Allah
for the blessings He bestowed upon me.

I'm not here to make others jealous, I'm not
here to make people feel lonely. I'm not here
to please creation or please my nafs.

I'm only here to please Allah.

s.hukr

Through His Eyes

Loving perfection is easy,
anybody can do it.

But let's see how many of us
choose to love people despite
their imperfections.

s.hukr

Through His Eyes

"Who are you?"

I said: I am traveller on a journey to my grave.

"Who is she?"

I said: She is a Slice of Paradise.

"Do you love her to death?"

I said: Speak of her over my grave and
watch how she brings me back to life.

s.hukr

Through His Eyes

She showed me her beauty and expected me to approach her, but I turned a blind eye and ignored her.

She came back and said, "Am I not beautiful?" so I said, "Yes, you are very beautiful, but God has reserved me for someone else, you are not mine to touch."

She walked away confused as if she never faced rejection before. Pondering at how she still had respect for a man who told her "No".

I later found out that she had converted to Islam. When they told me about her story, they said, a faithful man reminded her of God in such a way that she cried all night until she found Islam.

s.hukr

Through His Eyes

I just wanna build my empire now and help people as best as I can. Leave this world better than how I found it.

s.hukr

Through His Eyes

Love people in such a way that your love is pure. It is not a desperate or needy type of love, nor does your love vary by how much someone loves you back.

Love people purely for the sake of Allah and watch how your love (with time) travels to their hearts.

s.hukr

Through His Eyes

If you catch my eyes, I'll give you
a smile in return. But if you make
my heart smile, ill melt your heart
until it flows like honey.

s.hukr

Through His Eyes

I've never actually had a celebrity crush
because I can't crush on someone based
solely off their looks, I just don't find people
attractive like that.

But a woman who has the ability to catch
my attention with her mindset and her
personality, has probably already
won my heart.

s.hukr

Through His Eyes

Kind loving words make a woman's heart move but ever wondered what makes a man's heart move?

s.hukr

Through His Eyes

I don't want your money,
your time is more valuable.

I don't want your gifts,
your Dua is more valuable.

I don't want your eyes,
I only want passage to
your heart.

So I can win it every day.

s.hukr

Through His Eyes

Is it weird if I wake up in the
middle of the night, with ache
in my heart and I remember you?

I miss seeing you, I miss spending time with
you. I miss everything about you.

I long for you, even if you
aren't longing for me.

s.hukr

Through His Eyes

Have you ever met a soul so sweet
that whenever you see them your
heart smiles?

Nothing else matters when you are
in the presence of someone
who is loved by God.

s.hukr

Through His Eyes

You live near the sea and
I live near the mountains.

You watch the sunsets
while I watch the sunrise.

You live far away but one
day we shall meet.

I will read your eyes and
forget about the sky.

You will hold my hand
and forget about the moon.

s.hukr

Through His Eyes

Most men do not ask for much. We just
want to come home to a genuine smile
and some warm food.

In return, we will provide safety, comfort and
affection. We will love you and take care of
your ever need according to our best ability.

We just want a wife that we adore
and who completes us. I hope
that isn't too much to ask.

s.hukr

Through His Eyes

Being a man isn't easy and I feel sad for the men that come home after a heavy and long day. Only to be met with a lack of love, respect and kindness.

Be the kind of woman, that the men in your life look forward to meeting. Whether it be your brother, husband or father. Show them love through a simple hug or smile. Let them forget the harshness of Dunya by spending quality time with them.

Be there for the men in your life. Remember, behind every good man is a good woman.

s.hukr

Through His Eyes

In your love, I learn how to love.
In your beauty, I learn how to
make poems.

You radiant my heart with
your light, but sometimes,
all I think about is her.

s.hukr

Through His Eyes

She thought she was independent
and strong, but she got one small
taste of love and she was hungry
for more.

She realised her life was more
beautiful with a man by her side.

s.hukr

Through His Eyes

I wanna come home to eyes
that smile at me and hands
that hug me into comfort,
that make me forget about
my long tiring day.

I want some nice warm food,
then we can pray and remember Allah.

Towards the night, I'm all yours,
ice cream or Netflix? Should I make
you laugh, or should I make you smile?

Or do you trust me to make those
eyes twinkle brighter than the night sky?

s.hukr

Through His Eyes

Gossip about me and Imma
take all your good deeds.

You have been warned :)

s.hukr

Through His Eyes

Some girls want your money,
some want your last name,
and others just want love.

Choose wisely.

s.hukr

Through His Eyes

A man who writes a book knowing
he will benefit at least **one soul** that
he will never meet, has begun to
understand the meaning of life.

s.hukr

Through His Eyes

I feel that people don't understand young men.
They are often neglected by society.

Either they are too spoiled by the parents or
neglected outright. Both of which are harmful.

Often, they need our support, love and guidance.

Someone who can listen to them.
Someone who can care for them.
Someone who will pray for them.

Being a young man in the modern world, is not
easy. It's incredibility difficult especially when
your father wasn't the best role model.

Women need to understand that not every man is
lustful. Not all men have bad intentions. They
might have flaws and shortcomings but don't
we all?

s.hukr

Through His Eyes

Men who have built empires
with only ideas of divine change,
are amongst the greatest lovers
of this world.

s.hukr

Through His Eyes

If you die tomorrow, ask yourself,
what did you leave behind?

Will people benefit from
your departure?

s.hukr

Through His Eyes

You fall in love with the little things
about her, like the sound of her mind
and the way she smiles.

s.hukr

Through His Eyes

Some women don't understand
how precious they could be.

s.hukr

Through His Eyes

Society needs to stop making marriage
harder than it needs to be.

Islam makes it easy but yall make
it harder just to satisfy your culture.

Stop it. I'm sick of "Muslims"
who commit shirk.

Worship Allah like
you mean it.

s.hukr

Through His Eyes

She asked me, why do you love me so much?

I smiled and thought about it.
I told her in way she would understand.

I said, honey, how can I not love someone who
reminds me of paradise every morning and is
the reason for my happiness in the evening?

I can't imagine a life without you. I love you,
because you are beautiful in every way imaginable.

You are the queen of my heart. You are a blessing
from Allah and I don't need anybody else but you.

s.hukr

Through His Eyes

She said:
I love your books.

I replied:
You love my books,
but you don't love me.

She smiled and told me,
if you had 3 wives,
I would still marry you.

s.hukr

Through His Eyes

Thank you for reading this book.

I hope that you enjoyed it and
found some joy from my words.

May Allah always mercy on you
and guide you towards the straight
path. **Ameen.**

Sincerely,
s.hukr

*P.S If you love my books, please promote them and share it
with others and maybe I'll write another one...*

202

S.hukr Books

1. Fajr and Noor

2. Through His Eyes

3. Noor upon Noor

4. Slice of Paradise

'on Keynes UK
'n Content Group UK Ltd.
'040622100823
'JK00001B/4